Baseball's Great Managers

by
Tim Wall

Watermill Press

Printed in the United States of America

Illustrations by Jim Odbert

ISBN 0-89375-702-0

Contents

John McGraw: "Little Napoleon"... 5

Connie Mack: "The Philadelphia
Gentleman".................15

Wilbert Robinson: "Uncle Robbie"...26

Frank Frisch: "The Fordham Flash"..35

Branch Rickey: "The Mahatma".....45

Leo Durocher: "Leo the Lip".......53

Casey Stengel: "The Old Professor"..66

Earl Weaver: "The Bantam Rooster".76

Billy Martin: "Billy the Kid".......86

John McGraw "Little Napoleon"

John McGraw will always be remembered as the first of the great baseball managers. Some say he was the greatest ever. Many fans, however, have forgotten what he did as a player.

McGraw played third base with the old Baltimore Orioles. The Orioles were

John McGraw

one of the best teams of the early days of baseball. They won by being smarter, rougher, and faster than anyone else.

Besides McGraw, they had stars such as Wee Willie Keeler. Keeler, McGraw, and the other Orioles were not known for hitting home runs. They *were* known for being able to hit the ball past the other team's fielders. This was called "hitting them where they ain't." The Orioles were also wonders at fielding and running the bases.

McGraw hit .334 over sixteen years of play. No one who has played third base has hit better, year in and year out. In 1899 he hit .391. Not until George Brett hit .392 in 1980 has a third baseman had a better season.

McGraw had a favorite way of getting on base. The ground in front of home plate in the Baltimore park was

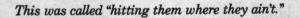

This was called "hitting them where they ain't."

kept as hard as a rock. When the pitch came, McGraw would chop at it with his bat. The ball would bounce off the hard ground and over the heads of the fielders. This type of hit became known as a "Baltimore Chop."

Of all the Orioles, McGraw was the smartest and the roughest. In 1899, while still playing third base, he was made manager of the team.

In 1902, Andrew Freedman, owner of the New York Giants, hired McGraw to be his manager. The Giants had an awful team. For years they had been in last place.

McGraw's first act was to fire ten of the Giants' 24 baseball players.

"What are you doing to my ball club?" Freedman asked McGraw.

"We can finish in last place with 14 men just as easily as with 24," McGraw told him.

He was right. In 1902, the Giants again finished in last place.

But McGraw began building up the team. He brought in new players. He taught all of them the basics of the game. No one knew hitting, running, and fielding better than McGraw.

Most of all, McGraw taught his team to win. The Giants played exciting baseball. They scratched and clawed for each run. They insulted the players on the other team. They even fought for each other.

The next year, the Giants finished in second place. The year after, they were in first. From that time on, the Giants were nearly always at the top or near the top.

He taught them the basics of the game.

McGraw's players began calling him "Little Napoleon." They named him after the great French general because McGraw was a short man and because he ran his team the way a general runs an army. He drilled them like soldiers. He told them exactly where to play in the field. When they were at bat, he told them when to swing and where to hit the ball.

McGraw asked the most from his players. But he never asked more than he knew he could do himself.

Sometimes the young players would say he was asking them to make plays that were impossible. Then McGraw himself would take the field. The old man showed them how to make the play they thought couldn't be done.

McGraw was especially good with pitchers. Christy Mathewson and Carl

Hubbell pitched for him. Burleigh Grimes came to the Giants after he had been pitching for eleven years. "McGraw taught me more about pitching in the first fifteen minutes than I learned in eleven seasons," he said.

McGraw was a baseball manager for 33 years. His Giants finished in first place ten times. No other manager has finished first more often.

By 1932 McGraw was an old man, and sick. The Giants were in sixth place. McGraw did not like losing. On top of that, the game of baseball had changed. The new heroes were home-run kings like Babe Ruth, Lou Gehrig, and Jimmie Foxx. The art of stealing bases, of the hit-and-run, was on the way out.

McGraw called Bill Terry into his office. Terry played first base for the

Giants. He was one of their all-time hitting stars.

"How would you like to be the new manager of the Giants?" McGraw asked him.

The switch was made. The next year the Giants, under Terry, were back in first place.

Even at the very end, the "Little Napoleon" knew how to make the right move.

Connie Mack "The Philadelphia Gentleman"

In 1886, the Washington Nationals signed a new catcher named Cornelius McGillicuddy. The young man came from a poor family. He tried baseball only because he had lost his factory job.

Later on, he told his father that he was going to become a ball player.

Connie Mack

"I guess it's all right," his father said. "But why don't you get into something that's lasting?"

Mr. McGillicuddy needn't have worried.

His son, whose name was soon shortened to "Connie Mack," stayed in baseball for sixty-six years. For sixteen years, he was a catcher. For fifty years, he was manager and part-owner of the Philadelphia Athletics. When he finally left the game in 1950, he was eighty-eight years old.

In Connie Mack's early days, baseball was a young sport, and a wild one. The players didn't make much money, and more than a few of them were known to be somewhat wild when they were off the playing field. They didn't act much better *on* the playing field either.

If an umpire was not liked, the players often ganged up on him and knocked him to the ground. Gamblers paid team members to "throw" ball games. Taking note of all this, many hotels refused to let ball players inside their doors.

Connie Mack stood out from the other baseball men of the time. He was well mannered. He was firm, but always polite. As a manager, he wore a suit and straw hat to every game. On very hot days, he would take off his coat and tie and watch the game in his shirt sleeves. The tall, thin manager in the straw hat became one of the best known sights in baseball.

In those years, most of the players were used to being called names like "Bloody Jake," "Dirty Jack," and "Wahoo Sam." Connie never used any

He wore a suit and straw hat to every game.

19

such names. When he spoke to his players, he addressed them as "Mister," and then said their last name.

It wasn't that Connie wouldn't use a trick or two himself. As a catcher, he learned how to pull at a hitter's bat just before the pitch came in. The angry batter would turn and stare at him. Connie, always the perfect gentleman, would say he was sorry. He told the batter in his soft voice that it had been a careless mistake. By this time, the hitter was so angry he was lucky if he didn't strike out.

But most of all, Connie Mack believed that baseball was a game of skill and of thinking. He did more than anyone else to make that idea real.

He worked to chase the gamblers out of baseball. He hired scouts to search the country for the best young ball players. And he showed his players the best ways to use their skills.

Connie was at his best when teaching young pitchers the secrets of their art. He had learned how to handle pitchers during his years as a catcher. With the Athletics, he trained some of the best pitchers of baseball's early years. Among them were Eddie Plank, "Chief" Bender, Herb Pennock, "Bullet Joe" Bush, "Lefty" Grove, and "Rube" Waddell.

The way Connie's players saw it, there was only one fault with their manager. He wasn't free enough in spending the club's money.

They may have had a point.

By 1910, the Athletics had been built into one of the smoothest winning-machines in the history of baseball. The stars of their infield were the pride of Philadelphia. They were called the "$100,000 Infield." This was the total amount of money made by the group of four players.

Mack felt the team had become too high-priced.

He sold off his stars, and started over with young, unknown players. For the next seven years, the Athletics finished in last place.

Mack tried out the new players with care. Finally, he sorted them out into a winning team.

Led by Jimmie Foxx and Al Simmons, the Athletics won pennants in 1929, 1930, and 1931. It was said that Foxx and Simmons were a match for the other great hitting team of the time, Babe Ruth and Lou Gehrig.

Again, Mack decided it was time to sell off his stars. Another winning-machine was taken apart.

For almost twenty years he worked to build another great team, but without luck. When he left baseball in 1950, his Athletics were in last place.

Mack will always be remembered, however, for the teams he put together in the early part of the 1900s. Those teams won nine pennants for Connie. Only John McGraw and, in later years, Casey Stengel, ever won more.

Mack is also remembered for the way he could handle even the wildest baseball players. And he had some wild ones.

One of his finest pitchers was Rube Waddell. Waddell was a player who seemed to prove the story that all left-handed pitchers are more than a little bit crazy.

It was Rube's boyhood dream to be a firefighter. At the sound of a fire alarm or a fire engine he would drop what he was doing. He would even leave the field in the middle of a baseball game. Later on, he would be found in a fire hat and coat, helping to put out the blaze.

Even with this kind of behavior, Mack remained calm. No matter what happened, he never lost his temper.

When he left baseball in 1950, it seemed hard to believe that the tall, quiet man in the straw hat would not be directing any more games at the ball park in Philadelphia. For fifty years, he had taught baseball to some of the best players the game has known. And most of the all-time greats that didn't play for Connie were on the teams that faced the Athletics.

From Ty Cobb to Joe DiMaggio, Connie Mack saw them all.

Wilbert Robinson
"Uncle Robbie"

Wilbert Robinson started in baseball as a catcher for the Baltimore Orioles. When John McGraw became the team's manager in 1899, Wilbert became his coach. And, when McGraw left to manage the New York Giants in 1902, Robinson went with him as his coach.

Wilbert Robinson

There came a day, however, when the two friends fought. McGraw said Robinson had missed one of his signs. Robinson said McGraw flashed the wrong sign, and the coach refused to take the blame.

Charlie Ebbets, the owner of the Brooklyn Dodgers, saw his chance. He signed Robinson to manage his team.

In Robinson's days with the rough-and-ready Orioles, he had been lean and fast. He was a quick base-runner and a sharp hitter. In one game with the Orioles he slammed seven hits in seven at-bats, a record that still stands.

By the time Robinson was the Brooklyn manager, he was a good deal older and wiser. He was also as big-hearted as he was round. Damon Runyon, the great newspaper man, wrote that Robinson looked like "your Uncle

He was a quick base-runner and a sharp hitter.

Wilbert." The name stuck. Later he was also called "The Round Robin," or "Uncle Robinson," or just "Uncle Robbie."

Robinson remained the Brooklyn manager for eighteen years. In that time, his team was called the "Robins," in his honor.

Under Uncle Robbie's gentle rule, the Robins were one of the oddest teams in all of sports. One day their dashing play would drive their fans wild with joy. The next day a silly mistake would lose the game and the fans would be broken-hearted.

There was Dazzy Vance, a pitcher with blazing speed. Dazzy wore the same shirt every time he pitched. He said it brought him luck. Of course, it didn't hurt that the sleeves, cut into strips and flapping in the breeze, made it hard for enemy hitters to follow his pitches.

There was also Casey Stengel. His boasting and clowning made him a favorite in Brooklyn.

Perhaps the most bird-brained Robin of all was Babe Herman. There was no question about Herman's hitting. In all his years in baseball he hit .324. One year with Brooklyn he hit .393.

But somehow, Babe never failed to find new ways to make life hard for his manager. With Babe in the field, each fly ball was an adventure. One of them bounced off his head.

Babe's finest hour came during a game when he was at bat with the bases loaded. He sent a shot to the center-field wall.

The runner on second thought the ball might be caught. He left the base late. When he rounded third it looked like he might be nailed at the plate.

31

He returned to third, only to find the runner from first base already there.

All the while Babe was running, head down, thinking of the big hit he had just made. He steamed into third base, and now there were three Robins on the bag.

The Robins had turned Babe's hit into a double play. The fans groaned.

Casey Stengel tried to defend Babe and the rest of Robbie's team.

"These things happen because we're all hitters," he said. "Unless we could hit there would not have been more than one man on third at a time. Any time you show me a team with three runners on third, that's the team for me."

The Brooklyn Dodgers were as different from the New York Giants as

...and now there were three Robins on the bag.

Wilbert Robinson was different from John McGraw.

McGraw's Giants were the most feared team in baseball. Their ball park was in Manhattan, and the rich and powerful were among their fans.

The Dodgers were more of a neighborhood team. People in Brooklyn would stop Robinson in the street to tell him how to handle his team. Even Robbie's wife told him which pitchers to use.

Although he had some odd players to work with, Robinson twice led the Dodgers to the pennant. It was clear he was one of the smartest baseball men around. What's more, for eighteen years he brought together teams that were as funny as they were exciting.

Frank Frisch
"The Fordham Flash"

In 1926, there were two great second basemen in baseball. Rogers Hornsby—the "Rajah"—was with the St. Louis Cardinals. Frank Frisch played second for John McGraw's Giants.

Frisch came to the Giants straight from Fordham University, where he had starred in track, football, and base-

Frank Frisch

ball. Few players in those days had been to college. Fewer still could hit, run, and field like Frisch. It wasn't long before he was called "The Fordham Flash."

Frisch was the kind of player McGraw liked. He was smart, he was fast, and he played to win. McGraw made him the team captain.

It was believed that Frisch would someday follow McGraw as the Giants' manager. However, both men were strong-willed. They couldn't work together. McGraw decided to trade Frisch away.

Meanwhile, in St. Louis, where Hornsby was player-manager, there also were problems. Hornsby refused to take orders from the team's owner. He also said he wasn't being paid enough.

Sam Breadon, the owner of the St.

*He was smart, he was fast, and he played
to win.*

Louis team, and Branch Rickey, its general manager, decided Hornsby had to go. He was traded to New York for Frisch.

The fans were upset and angry when they learned that Hornsby had been traded. Sam Breadon's home and business were damaged by angry citizens. He was attacked in the newspapers.

Luckily, Breadon was saved by the Fordham Flash. The way Frisch played made the fans forget all about Hornsby. He sliced hits to all parts of the field, and ran the bases as if he owned them. In 1927, with the Cardinals, Frisch stole more bases than anyone else in baseball. In 1930, he was voted the most valuable player.

A few years later, Frisch was named the Cardinals' manager. He managed the Cardinals for six years.

He was the manager for other teams for ten more years. His best year, however, came in 1934. That was his first full season as the Cardinals' leader.

The Cardinals were then known as the "Gas House Gang." They were such a high-spirited group, they would play a joke on anyone.

One of their tricks was dropping bags of water from hotel windows. Frisch himself suffered a few near-misses. Another favorite was to sprinkle visitors with sneezing powder.

As pitchers, the Cardinals had the brother act of Dizzy and Daffy Dean. Daffy was actually very quiet. Dizzy, on the other hand, could boast as well as he could pitch, which was quite well. The two had grown up as poor farm workers in the nearby Ozark Mountains.

The power-hitter on the team was Joe Medwick. He was called "Ducky" because of the funny way he walked. Pepper Martin played third base. For fun, he drove racing cars. Martin teamed up with the Dean brothers to lead an off-key country music band.

Rounding out the infield was Leo Durocher. He was known as "Leo the Lip" because he would talk back to anyone. The money he made shooting pool helped to pay for his fancy clothes and his big, expensive cars.

Frisch had his problems with the "Gas House Gang." In July of 1934, the Dean brothers went on strike for several weeks to get more money. In September, right in the middle of the pennant race, Durocher took time off to get married.

Frisch was perhaps the only man who could have held such a team together. Most of the time he went along with the joking. When he had to, though, he laid down the law. All the same, the 1934 season put a few gray hairs on his head.

The Cardinals beat out Bill Terry's Giants for the pennant on the last day of the season. They faced the Detroit Tigers in the World Series.

The Dean brothers, who had won forty-nine games in the regular season, kept on winning. But the hard-hitting Tigers kept coming back to match the Cardinals.

Frisch named Dizzy Dean to pitch the final game. It was sure to be close. Dean might have been the best pitcher in baseball, but he was tired. He had pitched almost every other day since the last weeks of the season.

Also, Frisch was no longer the Fordham Flash of old. He was a few steps slower, and had not been hitting against the Tigers.

Neither team had scored when Frisch came to bat with runners on base. He knifed the ball straight through the infield.

"Look at that old Dutchman run!" shouted Pepper Martin.

Frisch was on second base, and three runs had come in. The Cardinals went on to score four more times before the Tigers could get the side out. The Cardinals ran away with the game. The final score was 11–0.

The Cardinals were world champions. And, it was widely agreed that only Frank Frisch could have taken them to the top.

Branch Rickey
"The Mahatma"

In 1934, the St. Louis Cardinals won the pennant. It was the fifth they had won in nine years. Between 1942 and 1946, they won four more.

It takes more than a few good players and a great manager for a team to win that many pennants. It takes the support of a strong organization.

Branch Rickey

The man who built the St. Louis organization was Branch Rickey. He signed the players and made the trades. As general manager, he had the last word.

New ball players came from the minor-league teams. These teams could be found in almost any small city. Young players signed with them, and hoped to be noticed by a big-league team.

Rickey came up with a way to make sure he could keep good young players coming to the Cardinals. He paid certain minor-league teams for the rights to their players. Then he sent his own coaches to teach them baseball.

Rickey called these teams his "farm system." His plan worked so well, the other major-league organizations eventually copied it.

Rickey was both admired and feared by the other teams. Some people said he was crooked. Some of his own players called him cheap. Everyone agreed he was a man who would get his own way.

After the Cardinals won the pennant in 1942, Rickey decided to try a new team. He became general manager of the Brooklyn Dodgers.

As expected, Rickey began to build up the Brooklyn farm system. His next move, however, was not expected.

He signed a man named Jackie Robinson to his Montreal farm team. Robinson was a good hitter and a daring base runner. He was also black.

At that time, black baseball players were not allowed on major-league teams. In 1888, the baseball owners had agreed to an anti-Negro rule. Ever since, blacks could play only in Negro leagues.

There had been many who were great players, of course. Josh Gibson was one of the most powerful hitters ever. Satchel Paige used to pitch against Dizzy Dean in the off-season and beat him.

Rickey thought it was time the "color line" was broken. Besides, he wanted good ball players.

In 1947, Robinson was brought up from Montreal to the Dodgers. No player has had a harder year than Robinson did in 1947. He was insulted in every city the Dodgers visited. The fans watched to see what mistakes he would make.

Rickey had known how hard it would be for Robinson. He also knew

Robinson had pride, and he had nerve. Rickey was as good a judge of people as he was of baseball.

Robinson answered the insults with his bat, his glove, and his daring steals of home.

Led by their young star, the Dodgers won the pennant in 1947. Two years later, Robinson was voted the league's Most Valuable Player. Again, the Dodgers finished first.

Rickey brought more black players to the Dodgers — Roy Campanella, Junior Gilliam, Don Newcombe. The Dodgers kept on winning. Once again, Branch Rickey had the strongest team in the National League.

The other teams, in both leagues, had no choice but to follow Rickey's lead. One by one, each club's color line was broken.

*Robinson answered the insults with his bat, his
glove, and his daring steals of home.*

It hadn't seemed possible a few years before. But Branch Rickey was a man who was used to doing things his own way.

Leo Durocher
"Leo the Lip"

Since the early 1900's, the New York Giants and the Brooklyn Dodgers had been bitter rivals. Each game between the two teams was fought as if it was a major battle.

So in 1947, when Leo Durocher became the manager of the Giants, the

Leo Durocher

baseball world was stunned. Durocher, after all, had been the Dodgers' manager for nine years. He had led them to the pennant in 1941. The Giants' fans couldn't believe that their old enemy was now the manager of their team.

Across the river, in Brooklyn, the Dodger fans were also shocked. Durocher managing the Giants? It was as if George Washington had been sent to fight for the British.

Causing shock waves was nothing new for Durocher. He had been doing it since he began playing baseball in 1928.

Leo Durocher came from Springfield, Massachusetts, where he was a factory worker. He liked to wear leather jackets, and he liked to talk big.

He could also play baseball. He joined the world champion New York Yankees in 1928. It didn't matter to him that the most famous heroes of the game played for the Yankees. He talked back to anyone and everyone.

The Yankees were soon calling him "Lippy" and "Leo the Lip." Due to his light hitting, they also gave him the tag "The All-American Out."

But Durocher's fielding was a different story. He is said to have had just about the quickest moves of anyone who ever played shortstop.

Branch Rickey, the general manager of the St. Louis Cardinals, brought Durocher to his team in 1933. Rickey had plans to make the Cardinals a first-place team again. He liked Durocher's fancy fielding as well as his fighting spirit.

Durocher fit right in with the rough-and-ready Cardinals. He played beside the great second baseman, Frank Frisch.

But Durocher's fielding was a different story.

In 1934, the "Gas House Gang" from St. Louis won the World Series, and Durocher was one of their stars.

He became manager of the Brooklyn Dodgers in 1939. A few years later, Branch Rickey joined the club as general manager. Over the course of the 1940's, the Dodgers became the most powerful team in the National League.

As a manager, Durocher was always ready to trade insults or punches with the players from the other teams. And he never had a kind word for an umpire. This led to Leo being thrown out of more than a few ball games.

In one game, the head umpire made a call Leo didn't agree with. He called the umpire a long list of nasty names. The umpire told him to take a shower.

The next day, Durocher took his line-up card to home plate before the game began. The same umpire took the card from him.

"Do you remember what I called you yesterday?" Leo asked him.

"Yeah," the umpire said.

"Well, the same still goes for today."

"You're out of the game!" returned the umpire.

Durocher's remarks to the newspapers got him into trouble as well. In 1947, the league president took him out of baseball—not for one game, but for the whole season.

When Durocher went from the Dodgers to the Giants in 1948, he knew that some changes would have to be made. The Giants were not his kind of team. They had big, heavy men who could pound the ball. But they couldn't run or field very well. They hit lots of home runs and lost lots of ball games.

Durocher talked the Giants' owner, Horace Stoneham, into making some trades. Eddie Stanky and Alvin Dark, who played the infield much the same way Durocher had, were brought on. A few more big men were sent away for better pitchers. In 1951, Durocher pulled in a young player from one of the Giants' farm teams. The player's name was Willie Mays.

Durocher was known as a tough manager. But many of his players also saw his warmth and knew that he cared about them. They said he could get the best from each man that played for him. Willie Mays was a case in point.

Mays became one of the greatest players baseball has ever known. He had as much fun playing the game as the fans had watching him. But, when Willie first came to the Giants, he was just a thin, shy kid from Alabama. He wasn't used to the big leagues, or the big city. He would go for days without getting a hit. Willie was worried.

Durocher took the youngster under his wing. He taught him all he knew from his years in baseball. He cheered him up when he had a bad game. During Willie's first year with the Giants, Durocher called his apartment every day to ask how he was doing.

Late in the season, in 1951, the Dodgers were far ahead of any other team in the National League. Branch Rickey had brought the best players to the Dodgers, and they were everybody's favorites to win the pennant.

Durocher, however, sensed victory. He had the kind of team he wanted. As Willie Mays caught fire, so did the rest of the Giants. In August, they ran up a string of sixteen straight wins. The Dodgers' lead was narrowed, and they were running scared.

Durocher paced back and forth at the games. On the train, when his team was traveling, he kept repeating to his players, "We're going to win. We're going to win."

When the season ended, the Dodgers and the Giants were in a tie for first place. A three game play-off was set up to decide the pennant.

The Giants won the first game, but the Dodgers took the second. In the final game, the Dodgers held a 4–1 lead in the ninth inning. Everyone in New York, it seemed, was either at the ball park or listening to the game on the radio.

The Giants came through with three hits in the bottom of the ninth. One run scored, and two Giants were on base. The Dodgers brought in a new pitcher. Bobby Thomson stepped to the plate for the Giants.

Thomson lined the second pitch into the left-field stands.

In every corner of New York, radios blared with the announcer's voice: "The Giants win the pennant! The Giants win the pennant!"

It wasn't the first time Durocher had led a team to the pennant. And it wouldn't be the last. In 1954, his Giants, led by Willie Mays, again topped the National League. They went on to beat the Cleveland Indians in the World Series, four games to none.

But the 1951 victory over the Dodgers was Durocher's favorite win. Years later, sportswriters would vote Bobby Thomson's home run the most exciting moment in baseball history.

"The Giants win the pennant!"

Everyone knew Durocher could talk big. In 1951, he proved, for once and for all, he could put together the team to back it up.

Casey Stengel
"The Old Professor"

In 1948, Bucky Harris was fired as manager of the New York Yankees.

The new manager was a man with ears that stuck out from his head, a nose like a bulb, and bow legs. His name was Charles Dillon "Casey" Stengel.

Casey Stengel

Casey knew he had his work cut out for him. Harris had been well liked by the New York fans and players. Many of the champion players of the Yankees were against Casey from the start. Many writers said he wasn't "high class" enough for the proud Yankee team.

In his youth, Casey was better known for his clowning than for his playing. He hit well and was a smart fielder. But Casey was always looking for a laugh.

One day he stood completely still in center field. Finally, his manager came out to ask him what was wrong.

"I'm too weak to move," Stengel told him. "I'm not able to feed myself on what this club is paying me."

During another game, Casey's team was playing at a field where the crowd was known to be unfriendly. Before the game, Casey found a wounded sparrow. He placed it under his cap.

When Casey took the field, the fans began to boo him. Casey tipped his cap. Out flew the sparrow. The boos of the surprised crowd turned to cheers.

Casey learned to joke around while playing with the old Brooklyn Dodgers. But he also learned baseball. He learned even more when he was traded to the New York Giants. There he had the great John McGraw for a manager.

When Stengel's playing days were over, he became a manager. He led the Brooklyn Dodgers from 1934 to 1936 and the Boston Braves from 1938 to 1943. The players of both teams, however, were mostly over the hill. Neither team won many games. As often happens, many people blamed the manager.

Casey tipped his cap.

One year, a Boston cab driver hit Casey by accident. A local sports writer voted the driver "the man who did the most for Boston in 1943."

But no matter how bad his teams were, Casey never lost his sense of humor.

Near the end of one game it became very dark. There were no lights in those days. Eager to avoid a loss, Casey asked for the game to be called off. It wasn't. Casey went out to talk with his pitcher. In his hand, he carried a flashlight. Casey made his point.

After his team had lost several games in a row, Casey went to a barbershop. "A shave, please," he said. "And don't cut the throat. I might want to do that myself."

So when Casey came to the Yankees, there were many who didn't believe in him.

The pennant race was close in 1949. The Yankees won it from the Boston Red Sox on the last day of play.

Stengel knew he couldn't let up. Many of the great Yankee stars were getting old. Joe DiMaggio, Phil Rizzuto, and King Kong Keller would leave the team in a few years. Younger talent was needed.

He worked hard with the young players from the Yankee farm teams. He taught the basics just as John McGraw had done fifty years before. Under Stengel's direction, stars such as Mickey Mantle, Whitey Ford, Billy Martin, and Yogi Berra were given their start.

Casey was called "The Old Professor." The title might have come from his long talks with sportswriters. These talks were as funny as they were wise. The writers loved them. But Stengel was also "The Old Professor" because of the way he could teach baseball.

Casey's young stars played their hearts out for him. The mighty Yankees continued their winning streak and went on to win four more pennants. That brought their total to five pennants in a row. No other manager has been able to put together a string of pennants that long. From 1949 to 1953, the Yankees were on top.

In 1954, the Yankees had another good year. They won 103 games. But the Indians were better. They won 111, setting an all-time record.

Under Stengel, the Yankees came roaring back.

Under Stengel, the Yankees came roaring back. They won pennants in 1955, 1956, 1957, 1958, and again in 1960.

Millions still laughed with Casey and his jokes. But no one would ever laugh *at* him again. He had won ten pennants in only twelve years!

His ten pennants equalled the number won by John McGraw himself. Casey's Yankees won the World Series seven times. The Yankee fans couldn't have asked for more.

When Casey played baseball with the Dodgers and the Giants, he had been a favorite with the fans. Now, once again, he was the toast of New York.

Earl Weaver
"The Bantam Rooster"

Which baseball team has won the most games in recent years? The New York Yankees? The Los Angeles Dodgers? The Cincinnati Reds?

The answer is the Baltimore Orioles. And the manager who led his team to the most wins over that period is Earl Weaver.

Earl Weaver

Weaver never received much national attention until 1979. That year the Orioles were in the World Series, and he was voted "Manager of the Year."

Winning was nothing new for Weaver. In thirteen years, his Orioles finished either first or second a total of eleven times. Between 1969 and 1971, he won three pennants in a row, and over one hundred games each season.

What's more, he won with a club that never was able to pay millions of dollars for its players.

Weaver's teams depend on organization more than they do on a handful of stars. During spring training, Weaver works with his players on all parts of the game—which base to throw to on each kind of hit, how to bunt to advance a base runner, how to bunt for a base hit.

Earl is a judge of what a baseball player can do, but also of what a baseball team needs. He matches the kinds of players he has, and where they are played, to what his team needs.

Weaver selects the line-up for each game with care. He says this is the most important job a manager has. Weaver does not start the same players game after game. There is a different combination of Orioles on the field from one game to the next.

It seems Weaver always knows who has a hit in his bat, and who will make the big fielding play. Some people say he must use magic. Others think he's just lucky.

Weaver explains there's no magic

Records are kept of every game his team plays.

in it. His secret is statistics. Records are kept of every game his team plays. The records are stored in an old file cabinet. He knows which teams his pitchers do best against. He knows which of his hitters do best against enemy pitchers.

For all his use of statistics, Earl is not a dull manager. Ask any umpire. Or better yet, watch Earl when a close call goes against his team. He charges onto the field, waves his arms, kicks the dirt, throws his cap on the ground.

At one game he was so angry he walked off with third base. The police had to be sent to get it back.

The umpires, of course, always win the arguments. They don't enjoy Earl's acting as much as the Baltimore fans do. In fact, they would rather just throw

*The umpires, of course, always win
the arguments.*

him out of the game. And they've done just that on a number of occasions.

However, even though Earl loses the arguments, he keeps on winning the games.

Earl first became interested in baseball when he was a young boy. This, of course, didn't make him much different from millions of other American boys. But Earl had an inside view of the game most boys don't have.

His father ran a laundry business in St. Louis. One of the laundry's customers was the St. Louis ball club, the Cardinals. Earl's job after school was to pick up the dirty uniforms from the ball park and take back the clean ones. He was able to talk with players that most other people only saw from the stands.

Earl set his heart on becoming a big-league player himself. Even though he was short, and not very strong, he worked at learning the game. After he finished school, he was picked up by a minor-league team.

Weaver played shortstop for fourteen years in the minor leagues. His fielding was sharp, but he never hit very well. He never made it into a big league line-up.

All the time, though, he watched the managers and the other players. He saw how a smart manager could turn a game around with the right move in the late innings. By understanding what he himself couldn't do, he was able to understand the strong points and weak points of any player.

Weaver became known as a smart

baseball man. He was hired to manage several minor-league teams. In 1968, he got his chance with the Orioles. In 1969, he won his first pennant. He's been with the Baltimore club ever since.

Earl has taken his teams to the World Series four times. He's a figure that's known across the country, and a hero in the city of Baltimore.

"Good ball players make good managers, not the other way around," Earl says. "All I can do is help them be as good as they are."

He seems to have done a good job of it.

Billy Martin
"Billy the Kid"

A small group of men sat at a table, talking and drinking coffee. The lady waiting on the table recognized one of them. She knew him many years ago. He was a kid then. And he got into a lot of fights. His name was Manuel Alfred Pesano Martin. But everyone called him Billy.

Billy Martin

Billy Martin was back in his home town. But it had taken him a long time to get there.

Billy had grown up in the area, near the San Francisco Bay. It was a rough neighborhood. For most of the boys, life meant fights and gang wars when they were young. And, when they were older, it meant working and not knowing if their families would have enough for the next meal.

Billy was lucky. He could play baseball. When he finished school he was signed by the Oakland Oaks, the local minor-league team.

Billy was short and thin, and he played baseball the same way he fought. He made sure he was smarter and rougher than anyone else.

When Billy was playing for the Oaks, the team's manager was a man named Casey Stengel. Eventually, Stengel left Oakland to become the Yankee manager. Soon after, he sent for Martin to join the New York team.

Martin became one of the Yankee leaders. He was not one of the stronger hitters on the team. But he was at his best in the big games. During World Series play, he set several hitting records.

Martin was a favorite of Casey Stengel. The old man taught him many skills he himself had learned from John McGraw and Wilbert Robinson.

But Billy's habit of getting into fights on and off the field got him into trouble with the Yankee owners. He was traded away.

When he was through as a player, he was hired as manager by the Minnesota Twins. In 1968, the Twins were a

He was at his best in the big games.

losing team. In 1969, Billy led them into first place. Then he fought with the club owners, and was fired.

It was the same story with the Detroit Tigers and the Texas Rangers. Martin never learned to get along with the team owners. Each time he built a winning club, he was fired.

Billy returned to New York in 1976. He brought the Yankees their first pennant in twelve years. The next year they won the World Series. This time Billy was fired not once, but twice.

Martin was picked up as manager by Charlie Finley, owner of the Oakland A's.

The A's were the same team that had played in Philadelphia under Connie Mack. The team had been moved to Kansas City and then to Oakland.

Oakland had a champion team for several years. But Finley felt his team had become too high-priced. He sold his best players.

The A's finished in last place in 1979. The experts said it was the worst team in baseball.

Billy was back in his home town. But it seemed like his team was a lost cause.

Over the winter, Martin and his coaches had a meeting. Together they planned for the next season.

The A's had some young pitchers who would do well if they were handled the right way. There weren't many strong hitters, but there were some youngsters who could run.

At spring training camp, the coaches drilled their young players. And, when the season opened, the A's

were a different team. They were playing tight baseball in the field. They ran
the bases like they owned them.

Martin had taught them some of
his trick plays. When the A's came
home to play in Oakland, they used one
of Martin's plays.

Runners were on first and third.
The man on first fell down as if he had
tripped. The other team's catcher, thinking he had an easy out, fired to first.

The runner on third, however, was
breaking for the plate. By the time the
surprised first baseman threw back
home, the run had already scored. By
this time the runner from first base was
sliding into second.

If the first baseman was surprised,
the Oakland fans were shocked. They
weren't used to baseball played this
well.

Suddenly, the ball park which had stood empty for so long was filling up with fans. They came to watch Billy Martin's brand of baseball.

The experts had picked the A's for last place in 1980. Instead, they finished second.

One of the many unknown players on the A's, Ricky Henderson, stole over a hundred bases. This broke the American League record that had been set 65 years before by the great Ty Cobb.

Martin was the only person in baseball who wasn't surprised by his team's showing. Billy Martin already knew he was a winner. He'd proved that years ago.